D0991517

NATIVE NATIONS OF THE
NORTHEAST

BY BARBARA KRASNER

RIVERHEAD FREE LIBRARY
330 COURT STREET
RIVERHEAD, NEW YORK 11901

The Child's World®

Published by The Child's World®
1980 Lookout Drive • Mankato, MN 56003-1705
800-599-READ • www.childsworld.com

Acknowledgments
The Child's World®: Mary Berendes, Publishing Director
Red Line Editorial: Editorial direction and production
The Design Lab: Design
Content Consultant: JoEllen Anderson, PhD, Native
American Studies Lecturer, University of California, Berkeley

Photographs ©: Arno Burgi/Picture-Alliance/DPA/AP
Images, cover, 2; Brooklyn Museum/Corbis, 1, 12; Shutterstock
Images, 3 (top), 14, 32; Joe Giblin/AP Images, 3 (middle top),
22; Library of Congress, 3 (middle bottom), 25; Stephan
Savoia/AP Images, 3 (bottom), 36; Red Line Editorial, 4; Rob
Rudeski/Shutterstock Images, 5, 39; Toby Talbot/AP Images,
6, 10; Kevin Wolf/AP Images, 8; Ken Sturm/US Fish and
Wildlife Service, 11; Ramin Talaie/Corbis, 16; Kevin Fleming/
Corbis, 18; Bradley C. Bower/AP Images, 19; Larry Wilder CC
2.0, 20–21; iStockphoto, 24; Marilyn Angel Wynn/Nativestock
Pictures/Corbis, 26; Sean D. Elliot/The Day/AP Images, 28;
David Tuttle/Shutterstock Images, 29; Aaron Flaum/The
Norwich Bulletin/AP Images, 30–31; Yuri Long CC 2.0, 34

Copyright © 2016 by The Child's World®
All rights reserved. No part of this book may be
reproduced or utilized in any form or by any means
without written permission from the publisher.
ISBN: 9781634070324
LCCN: 2014959803
Printed in the United States of America
Mankato, MN
July, 2015
PA02269

ABOUT THE AUTHOR

Freelance writer Barbara Krasner writes nonfiction,
fiction, and poetry for children and adults. She holds
an MFA in Writing for Children & Young Adults
from the Vermont College of Fine Arts and teaches
children's literature and creative writing at William
Paterson University in New Jersey, where she is
currently pursuing a master's in public history.

*Members of the
Oneida Nation
perform a dance.*

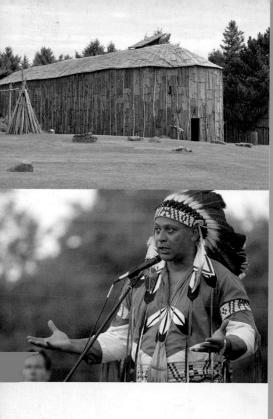

TABLE OF CONTENTS

ARCTIC

OCEAN

GREENLAND

Gulf of
Alaska

Hudson
Bay

PACIFIC

OCEAN

CANADA

ATLANTIC

OCEAN

UNITED STATES

KEY

NORTHEAST
NATIVE NATIONS

N
W E
S

MEXICO

Gulf of
Mexico

CHAPTER ONE

NATIVE NATIONS OF THE NORTHEAST

Elders tell the oral history of how Native Peoples have lived in the Northeast for thousands of years. The early peoples of the Northeast relied on the region's lush forests and plentiful lakes and rivers. Water gave them life. They farmed and

The Adirondack Mountains are the historic home of several Native Nations.

Abenaki tribe members sing and play drums in Montpelier, Vermont.

harvested their crops. They hunted and fished. To take advantage of seasonal food sources, some groups lived in one place during the summer and another place during the winter. Other groups stayed in one place year-round.

The Northeast region's western boundary touches the current midwestern states of Minnesota, Iowa, and Missouri. The eastern boundary ends at the Atlantic Ocean. The region extends as far north as the Canadian provinces of Ontario and Quebec, and its southern boundary reaches the states of Tennessee, Virginia, and North Carolina.

Historically, Northeast tribes often fought against each other for land and resources. Some groups formed long-lasting friendships that would protect them from attacks. One of these pacts was the Haudenosaunee **Confederacy**, also known as the Iroquois Confederacy, which was initially made up of five nations. Another confederacy, known as the Three Fires, brought together the Ojibwe, Ottawa, and Potawatomi.

Many nations have called the Northeast home. These groups include the Abenaki, Wampanoag, Narragansett, and Pequot in what is now known as New England. They also include the Haudenosaunee, mostly in New York, and the Lenape in the New Jersey area. The Powhatan of Virginia are also part of the Northeast nations. Groups such as the Ojibwe live in Minnesota, Michigan, North Dakota, Wisconsin, and parts of Canada.

Nearly every nation of the Northeast descends from one of two language groups: Algonquian-speaking and Iroquoian-speaking peoples. The Algonquians lived in **wigwams**. They farmed and fished. Men in Algonquian communities held more power than the women. The Haudenosaunee lived in **longhouses**. They farmed the Three Sisters: corn, beans, and squash. Women in Haudenosaunee communities held more power than men.

European settlement, war, and disease affected Native Nations differently. Only a few nations survived with their practices and language intact. Others had no choice

Two members of the Haudenosaunee Confederacy view a treaty at the National Museum of the American Indian. The treaty, written in 1794, was between the Haudenosaunee Confederacy and the United States.

but to live among the European settlers. Many children were sent to boarding schools far from home and forced to give up their traditions. Many nations of the Northeast have never regained their heritage. They no longer have speakers of their Native languages.

The loss of their people, lands, and traditions affected the ability of some Native groups to be **federally recognized** by the U.S. government. A few are state recognized but not federally recognized. Several Native groups continue to fight for federal recognition. Without federal recognition, they do not have tribal rights to hunt in the forests and fish in the waters. Without state or federal recognition, they cannot sell their arts and crafts such as beadwork and baskets. Federal recognition gives tribes **sovereignty**, or the right to govern themselves.

Several nations of the Northeast have legends about the origin of maple syrup. An Abenaki tale involves a man named Gluskabe. He found villagers lazing under the maple trees filling their mouths with maple sap. With instructions from the Creator, Gluskabe filled the trees with water. The villagers returned to their work. To remind them of their laziness, the trees would now produce this wonderful sap only once a year. They would use the sap to make a syrup they could enjoy year-round.

CHAPTER TWO

ABENAKI

Roger Longtoe Sheehan, an Abenaki chief, presents a pipe to Vermont governor Peter Shumlin.

The Abenaki are known as the People of the Dawn. They have two groups. The Eastern Abenaki live in Maine and southern Canada. The Western Abenaki live in Vermont, New Hampshire, and Massachusetts. Historically, the Abenaki moved about to take advantage of the best food supply. They lived in longhouses during the winter and wigwams during the summer.

The Abenaki fought against the Europeans and the Haudenosaunee to preserve their lands. Their population suffered from war and disease. They often sided with the French, but the French were defeated by Great Britain in 1763. Many remaining Abenaki moved to Canada, where their descendants now live on reservations. In the United States, only one band of the Eastern Abenaki, the Penobscot, has federal recognition. They live on a reservation in Maine. The other bands have no reservations.

Fishing remains part of Abenaki culture. One Abenaki band, the Missisquoi in Vermont, practices the art of ice fishing. The Abenaki use a special three-pronged fishing

Northern Vermont features wetlands that are home to many fish.

This Abenaki basket, made in the late 1800s, features an intricate swirling pattern.

Joseph Bruchac is a member of the Abenaki tribe. He has written more than 120 books for adults and children. He has also written poems, short stories, and music. Many of these works draw on his Native heritage. Bruchac carries on the Abenaki tradition of storytelling. He tells his stories at schools and festivals in the United States and around the world.

spear. The Missisquoi Bay offers plenty of perch, pike, and bass to catch.

The Abenaki are preserving parts of their traditional lifestyle. Today, people in the Elnu Abenaki band craft quillwork and shell beads. From time to time, they live as their ancestors did. For a few days each year, they live in wigwams, wear animal skins and wool, and tell stories. They return to modern life with a better understanding of their ancestors.

Like many northeastern Native languages, the Abenaki language belongs to the Algonquian family. Few, if any, fluent speakers remain. Communities are making efforts to bring back their language. Programs include online lessons and dictionaries.

SAY IT			
	one	pazekw	(pah-zuhk)
	two	nis	(nees)
	three	nas	(nahs)

HAUDENOSAUNEE

The Haudenosaunee (hoh-duh-nuh-SHOH-nee), also known as the Iroquois, are the People of the Longhouse. Six nations make up the Haudenosaunee Confederacy. They are the Mohawk, Oneida, Cayuga, Onondaga, Tuscarora, and Seneca. Most

A Haudenosaunee longhouse could be more than 300 feet (91 m) in length and had enough room to protect many families from harsh weather.

live on reservations in New York. The Oneida also have members living in Wisconsin. The Cayuga and Seneca have members living in Oklahoma as part of the Seneca-Cayuga Nation. These two groups were forced out of their traditional lands. Today they are involved in legal action in New York to regain land in Seneca and Cayuga counties.

In 1722, the Confederacy included its sixth nation, the Tuscarora. They are an Iroquoian-speaking people originally from North Carolina. Most members moved north to accept Haudenosaunee protection from the European colonists and other Native Nations in the area. The Tuscarora have a reservation in New York. However, the Southern Band of Tuscarora is not part of the Haudenosaunee Confederacy. They live in North Carolina.

The Haudenosaunee Confederacy has a population of more than 80,000 people in the United States and 45,000 in Canada. The Mohawk are the largest Haudenosaunee nation in New York, with more than 11,000 members. They run a casino, a hotel, and a spa. The Mohawk community at Kanatsiohareke in New York runs a farm. It also teaches visitors about the Haudenosaunee. The community offers many classes, including language immersion and workshops on Haudenosaunee culture and religion.

The Oneida have more than 16,000 members, mostly in Wisconsin. They own the Indian Country Today Media Network. The Oneida Nation Museum shows the tribe's art and daily life. The museum preserves their

The Iroquois Nationals lacrosse team competes in international competitions. In 2014, the team defeated Australia to win the bronze medal at the World Lacrosse Championship.

Onondaga men and women known as "faithkeepers" are responsible for making sure ceremonies are performed. They are busy all year round. Ceremonies celebrate midwinter, maple sap, planting, beans, strawberries, green corn, and the harvest. Faithkeeper Oren Lyons has traveled around the world speaking about the importance of protecting the environment.

history and culture for future generations. Traditional and modern works of art give visitors a glimpse of Oneida past and present.

The Seneca run two casinos, including one at Niagara Falls. Gaming is a big part of the Seneca economy. Few people speak the Seneca language today. For this reason, the Seneca Nation of Indians encourages students to learn their ancestors' language. Young children hear the language in the nation's preschool. The nation also sponsors language and culture classes. The nation wants children to grow up speaking the Seneca language so it is not forgotten.

The game of **lacrosse** is very important in Haudenosaunee culture. In the Native language, the game's name means "they bump hips." Lacrosse is a team sport in which each player has a stick with a small net at one end. Players try to score by shooting the ball into the opponent's goal. The Haudenosaunee use lacrosse as a way to bring communities together.

SAY IT

MOHAWK LANGUAGE

meat	o'wá:ron	(oh-wah-loh)
milk	onón:ta	(o-nohn-tah)
bread	kaná:taro	(kah-nah-ta-loh)

CHAPTER FOUR

LENAPE

A Lenape man dances at a powwow in Delaware.

The Lenape once lived throughout New Jersey, New York, Pennsylvania, and Delaware. The British called them the Delaware. The Lenape lived on Manhattan Island when the Europeans arrived there. In 1626, the Dutch gave the Lenape a

A member of the Lenape tribe takes part in an event to raise awareness about food safety.

small amount of trade goods, including items such as knives and clothing. The Lenape believed this payment allowed the Dutch to share their land. But the Dutch believed they had bought the land. The two groups lived in peace for a short time. However, European diseases took a heavy toll on the Lenape. By the early 1700s, the colonists had pushed the remaining Lenape out of their homeland.

U.S. government policies often forced Native Nations to relocate many different times. This was the case with the Lenape. Today, federally recognized Lenape nations have tribal headquarters in Oklahoma, Kansas, and Wisconsin. The Lenape also live on reservations in Canada.

Some Lenape live on traditional lands. The Nanticoke Lenni-Lenape live in southern New Jersey. They are a state-recognized tribe,

The Lenape Center is located on the ancestral Lenape island of Manhattan. Its mission is to promote Lenape language and culture. One of its projects is an opera called *Purchase of Manhattan*. This opera tells the story of the early encounters between the Lenape and the Dutch.

but they are not federally recognized. They maintain a 350-year-old friendship with Sweden, whose people settled in southern New Jersey before the British.

The Lenape place a high importance on education. They focus on teaching young people about Lenape culture so that it can be carried on through future generations. They also have a language program that provides textbooks, classes, and games to keep the language alive.

A boy dances at the Nanticoke Lenni-Lenape 2014 Powwow.

NARRAGANSETT

Matthew Thomas, chief of the Narragansett, speaks in favor of his tribe's right to sell tax-free goods.

Oral history and scientific evidence suggest the Narragansett nation dates back 30,000 years. Based in the Rhode Island area, the Narragansett spent summers living along the shore in wigwams. In the winter, they moved into longhouses.

English settlers killed many Narragansett in a war in 1675. Those who survived were moved to reservations. In the 1700s, they used much of this land to pay debts. In 1790, the U.S. government made it illegal to take land from Native Nations as payment for debts. But the state of Rhode Island ignored this law. In 1880, the state illegally took away the Narragansett's tribal status and land. Most members were scattered to nearby towns.

Through this hard time, the Narragansett continued coming together each year. They filed claims asking for their land back. Each attempt was rejected. They took legal action

The Narragansett hold an annual **powwow** to celebrate the two-day Green Corn Festival. The event has taken place for more than 300 years. Hundreds of tribal members and others come from all over the country to attend. The powwow hosts several dance contests for different age categories. There are also musical performers, traditional foods, and cultural events.

again in 1975. Three years later, they received land. They finally earned federal status as a tribe in 1983.

The Narragansett prepare and enjoy special foods that celebrate corn. These foods include **johnnycakes**, **succotash**, **Indian pudding**, and corn chowder. The Narragansett also prepare **quahog** chowder, which is made with a certain type of clam.

Members work to preserve the nation's land, water, and other resources. They also work to protect their ancestors' memories, history, and dwellings. In the past, roads were built without their participation. These roads destroyed many gravesites and culturally important places. The tribe set up a preservation office to make sure their history survives.

OJIBWE

Wigwams were typically meant to last for one season.

The Ojibwe, also known as the Chippewa, are one of the largest Native Nations in North America. They have 125 communities in Canada. They also have reservations in Michigan, Minnesota, Wisconsin, North Dakota, and Montana. Hundreds of

Five Ojibwe members ride in a canoe in 1913.

years ago, the Ojibwe banded together with the Ottawa and Potawatomi in the Council of Three Fires. Historically, the Ojibwe fought against the Haudenosaunee, also known as the Iroquois.

Today, more than 35,000 Ojibwe live on three reservations in Michigan. These reservations are Bay Mills, Grand Traverse, and Sault Ste. Marie. The Chippewa of Grand Traverse share their reservation with the

These Ojibwe mittens are made from moose hide and lined with beaver fur.

Ottawa. The Chippewa of Sault Ste. Marie, who have the largest of the three reservations, were originally from the Atlantic coast. All three reservations govern themselves. All three run casinos and hotels.

The Minnesota Chippewa have six bands. Most rely on casinos, hotels, and small businesses to bring money into their communities. But tradition is important, too. For example, the Mille Lacs Band of Ojibwe

knife	mookomaan	(moh-koh-mahn)
fork	badaka'igan	(bah-dah-kah-ee-gan)
spoon	emikwaan	(ey-meek-wahn)

SAY IT

are bringing new life to their language. *The Ojibwe People's Dictionary* is a resource that helps today's generation learn the language. The Ojibwe also started language immersion schools. Ojibwe children learn about subjects such as science and history in their ancestors' language. In addition, a group of women called the Swamp Singers sings in the Ojibwe language. They perform songs to drumbeats. The women hope their art preserves both language and culture.

The White Earth Reservation is the largest Native group in Minnesota. It is home to more than 19,000 members. The reservation installed equipment to harness wind power. The reservation also received a grant from the government to train residents in green technology.

A small Chippewa tribe of about 1,000 members lives in Wisconsin on the St. Croix Reservation. This group runs fisheries, a lumber company, and a clothing manufacturing company.

In December 2014, President Barack Obama selected the Sault Ste. Marie Chippewa as one of the 16 winners of the Climate Action Champions competition. The group works to manage energy and land use. It also helps keep the environment safe and clean. It serves as a role model for other communities.

CHAPTER SEVEN

PEQUOT

Pequot members dance while celebrating Connecticut Native American Heritage Month.

The Pequot, also known as the Fox People, have eastern and western tribes in Connecticut. In the 1600s, encounters with European settlers brought brutal killings to the Pequot. Many Pequot were forced into slavery far away from home.

Foxwoods Resort Casino towers above the surrounding countryside.

A small group of Pequot survivors stayed in Connecticut and found protection with the Eastern Nehantic people. This group became known as the Eastern Pequot. Others stayed in Connecticut but spent several years under the control of the Mohegan, a rival Native Nation. This group became known as the Western Pequot.

The Eastern Pequot reservation is one of the oldest in the United States. Colonial leaders created this reservation in 1683. Today, the Eastern Pequot continue their cultural heritage by hunting, farming, and making baskets. The Eastern Pequot are recognized by the state of Connecticut, but they are not federally recognized.

The Mashantucket Pequot Museum and Research Center aims to preserve Pequot culture. The museum conducts research and has programs about all Native Nations of the Northeast. Exhibits, films, and videos show the history of the Pequot. Visitors learn about daily life in a Pequot village and the arrival of the Europeans.

The Mashantucket, or Western Pequot, have about 800 tribal members. The Mashantucket are federally recognized. The tribe runs a casino, a golf course, and resorts. It is the largest employer in Connecticut. The casino is one of the largest in the world. The Mashantucket have contributed billions of dollars to Connecticut's local and state governments since the casino opened in 1992. The casino is the highest taxpayer in the state of Connecticut.

Mashantucket Pequot members celebrate Foxwoods Resort Casino's twentieth anniversary.

CHAPTER EIGHT

POWHATAN

A Powhatan woman takes part in a ceremony commemorating the 400th anniversary of the Jamestown settlement.

The Powhatan have lived in Virginia for more than 12,000 years. In the 1500s and 1600s, the Powhatan were a confederacy of 30 related Algonquian tribes. When the British arrived and settled at Jamestown in 1607, about 15,000 Powhatan lived in the area. But the tribe lost many members to new European diseases.

One of the most famous Powhatan is Matoaka, often called Pocahontas. In the early 1600s, a Powhatan man captured an English settler named John Smith. According to Smith's diary, Pocahontas helped save his life. Later, the English captured Pocahontas. She married an Englishman, John Rolfe, and he took her to England. There she became ill and died in 1617. Her son, Thomas, returned to Virginia. Today many of his descendants still live there.

Of the original 30 Powhatan Confederacy tribes, eight have received recognition from the state of Virginia. All of these tribes are trying to get federal recognition. Today the Powhatan number approximately 3,400 people. They mostly live in Virginia, but one band lives in New Jersey.

The Powhatan languages belong to the Algonquian family. For the most part, no one has spoken them for 300 years. But words have been found in historical documents, including John Smith's diary.

One Powhatan tribe, the Pamunkey, is well known for its pottery. Artists use centuries-old techniques, and they use mud from the Pamunkey River. In the 1930s, the Pamunkey set up a pottery-making business using money it received from the state of Virginia. The state also provided the building materials for a pottery school. Many students went on to become successful potters.

CHAPTER NINE

WAMPANOAG

Fire is being used to hollow out a Wampanoag boat at a living history museum in Massachusetts.

The Wampanoag are known as the People of the First Light. They are part of the Algonquian language family. Historically they lived in Massachusetts and Rhode Island. They lived in **wetus**, dome-shaped huts of grass and sticks. They relied

A Wampanoag man, right, gathers oysters in Mashpee, Massachusetts.

heavily on growing and harvesting the Three Sisters: corn, beans, and squash.

In the 1600s, they met the European settlers at Plymouth in present-day Massachusetts. At this time, the Wampanoag consisted of 69 tribes. They taught the settlers how to farm. However, the Wampanoag suffered greatly from European diseases. Later, many Wampanoag died in a war against the English colonists. These disasters wiped out 90 percent of their population. Groups isolated on the islands of Martha's Vineyard and Nantucket survived.

Today, the two major Wampanoag tribes are the Gay Head and the Mashpee. Both tribes are federally recognized. There are

Cedric Cromwell, chairman of the Mashpee Wampanoag, in his office

about 1,100 Gay Head tribal members. They live on a reservation on Martha's Vineyard. They run businesses that include gaming, tourism, and an environmental laboratory. The Mashpee live on Cape Cod and have about 2,600 tribal members.

Several Wampanoag communities are working together on a special project to restore their language. Like many Native groups during the 1800s, the Wampanoag were pressured to speak English and change religions. Children were not taught their Native language. In many Wampanoag families, no one has spoken the language for 100 years or more. In 2011, the Language Reclamation Project began a camp and a school for children. The project also offers classes for people of any age. More than 15 specially trained instructors teach these classes. It is the first Native language with no living speakers to be revived. One family is raising a child to speak Wampanoag as her first language.

The Wampanoag Environmental Laboratory is located on the southwestern shore of Menemsha Pond on Martha's Vineyard. Workers at the laboratory analyze drinking water and make sure it is safe for consumption. They also test soil and dust for the presence of lead. In addition, the laboratory shares information with the state and national governments. Lawmakers can then use this data when creating new environmental policies.

confederacy (kuhn-FED-er-uh-see) A confederacy is an alliance of groups banding together for a common purpose. The Haudenosaunee, the Ojibwe, and the Powhatan each formed a confederacy with other tribes.

federally recognized (FED-er-uhl-lee REK-uhg-nahyzd) When a tribe is federally recognized, it is entitled to certain rights and privileges from the U.S. government. A tribe with federal recognition receives money and services from the government to help its communities succeed.

Indian pudding (IN-dee-uhn PUD-ing) Indian pudding is a baked pudding made of cornmeal, molasses, milk, and spices. Indian pudding is a Native dish that celebrates corn.

johnnycakes (JOH-nee-keyks) Johnnycakes are a kind of bread made from fried cornmeal. Johnnycakes became part of early American food, but they started with the Native Nations.

lacrosse (luh-KRAWS) Lacrosse is a team sport in which players try to score goals by passing around a ball using long sticks with nets at the end. Today, people play lacrosse professionally and at many universities.

longhouses (LAWNG-hous-iz) Longhouses are homes where several families lived. The Haudenosaunee lived in longhouses.

powwow (POU-wou) A powwow is a gathering, meeting, or special ceremony. Many Native Nations host powwows to celebrate their cultures.

quahog (KOH-hog) Quahog is a kind of clam found in the coastal waters of the Atlantic Ocean. Quahog chowder is a favorite among the Narragansett.

sovereignty (SOV-rin-tee) Sovereignty is the independent power to govern. Tribal sovereignty grants Native Nations the right to govern themselves.

succotash (SUHK-uh-tash) Succotash is a mix of boiled whole kernels of corn, lima beans, and peppers. Succotash is a food of Narragansett origin.

wetus (WEE-tooz) Wetus are dome-shaped dwellings that look like wigwams. The Wampanoag once lived in wetus.

wigwams (WIG-womz) Wigwams are dome-shaped homes made with bark, skin, or mats wrapped around poles. Wigwams can stand up to bad weather thanks to their curved surfaces.

TO LEARN MORE

BOOKS

Johnson, Michael. *Native Tribes of the Northeast.* Milwaukee: World Almanac Library, 2004.

Kallen, Stuart A. *Native Americans of the Great Lakes.* San Diego: Lucent Books, 2000.

Kallen, Stuart A. *Native Americans of the Northeast.* San Diego: Lucent Books, 2000.

Kuiper, Kathleen, ed. *American Indians of the Northeast and Southeast.* New York: Rosen, 2012.

WEB SITES

Visit our Web site for links about Native Nations of the Northeast:

childsworld.com/links

Note to Parents, Teachers, and Librarians: We routinely verify our Web links to make sure they are safe and active sites. So encourage your readers to check them out!